The Little Gipper's

Welcome to NOTRE DAME FOOTBALL!

Written by Jacob Keyes, a 10-Year-Old Author & Avid Notre Dame Fan!

Graphic Design by Ellen Eide, Class of 2012, University of Notre Dame

ISBN-13: 978-0-615-65637-3

Limited use of the Play Like A Champion Today mark granted by PLACT, Inc.

Image and likeness of George Gipp used with permission by the Family of George Gipp by CMG Worldwide, www.CMGWorldwide.com

Photos reproduced courtesy of Notre Dame Archives unless otherwise indicated.

THE PLAYBOOK

ABOUT THE AUTHOR

Jacob Keyes is 10 years old and lives in Spokane, Washington with his parents and two younger sisters, Grace and Tess. Jake attends Cataldo Catholic School and, before that, he attended Southside Montessori and Children's House Montessori Schools. In addition to now being a young author, he is an accomplished pianist, chess player, and the quarterback and point guard on his football and basketball teams. One of his many big goals is to play football and basketball for his future high school, Gonzaga Prep, and then earn his way to South Bend to take the football field as a member of the Fighting Irish! Jake is inspired by the history and tradition of the University of Notre Dame and feels truly blessed and thankful to have been given so much encouragement and assistance from many others along the way in finishing this book. He hopes that this work will help inspire others to dream and to tackle big projects too! Now get out there and "Read One for The Little Gipper"!

"CHEER CHEER FOR OLD NOTRE DAME WAKE UP THE ECHOES CHEERING HER NAME!"

The author, Jacob Keyes, on his first night on Notre Dame's campus in 2010.

INTRODUCTION

The Little Gipper's® *Welcome to Notre Dame Football!* is a great way to learn about the University of Notre Dame and its world-famous football team! I began following Notre Dame football when I was seven years old and instantly became a huge and loyal fan. I was lucky enough to visit Notre Dame for a summer football camp when I was eight years old. I was so excited to be at Notre Dame that I stayed up until 2:00 a.m. that first night exploring the campus! I was just amazed at the shiny Golden Dome, the candlelight in the Grotto, the Basilica, the Hesburgh Library, and of course, Notre Dame Stadium (even in the dark!). In writing this book, I learned that Coach Lou Holtz once said this about Notre Dame: "If you've been there, no explanation is necessary. If you haven't, none is adequate." What I think this means is that Notre Dame is a very special place. It really is. Notre Dame truly inspires me and I wrote this book to help fans like me who want to learn more about the really cool traditions of this great University and its famous football team. I would love to hear from you if you have any comments or questions. I hope you enjoy this book as much as I enjoyed writing it. Go Irish!

that's me at age 2!

jake@littlegipper.com

IT'S NEVER TOO EARLY TO START DREAMING!

go irish! go irish! go irish! go irish! go irish! go irish! go irish! go irish! go irish! go irish!

CHAPTER ONE

The Fathers of Notre Dame Football

FATHER EDWARD SORIN
Founder, 1842

You might think it is curious that I would start this book about Notre Dame Football by mentioning the Rev. Edward Sorin, C.S.C., a Catholic priest from France. Fr. Sorin likely never played, coached, or probably even heard too much about the sport of football. But, if there were no Fr. Sorin, there would be no University of Notre Dame. So, I want you to know just a little bit about this great man.

In 1842, Fr. Sorin founded "L'Université de Notre Dame du Lac" (that's French for "The University of Our Lady of the Lake"). "Our Lady" is Mary, the Mother of Jesus. Fr. Sorin faced many obstacles in building Notre Dame, including a violent fire that destroyed almost the entire university in 1879.

But, he never gave up. Soon after the fire, Fr. Sorin said, "I came here as a young man and dreamed of building a great university in honor of Our Lady. But I built it too small, and she had to burn it to the ground to make the point. So, tomorrow, as soon as the bricks cool, we will rebuild it, bigger and better than ever." He sure did!

Fr. Edward Sorin, C.S.C.

KNUTE ROCKNE
1918–1931

Knute Rockne is one of the greatest coaches in the history of football. He was the head coach of Notre Dame's football team from 1918 to 1931. His football teams won three national championships in 1924, 1929, and again in 1930. Even though he coached a long time ago, his winning percentage as a head coach is still the best in all of college football! Rockne coached some very famous players in college football, including George Gipp and "The Four Horsemen." Knute Rockne was also much more than just a football coach, he was a brilliant scientist, salesman, business manager, and author of three books. He is also responsible for building Notre Dame Stadium (also known as "The House That Rockne Built"), where the football team still plays its home games today.

Before he was a coach, Knute Rockne actually played on Notre Dame's football team under Coach Jesse Harper. During his senior year, Knute Rockne played tight end where he caught many passes from his quarterback, Gus Dorais, and scored many touchdowns.

Tragically, Knute Rockne died in a plane crash over Bizarre, Kansas on March 31, 1931. He is buried in Highland Cemetery in South Bend, Indiana. Coach Rockne was inducted into the College Football Hall of Fame in 1951.

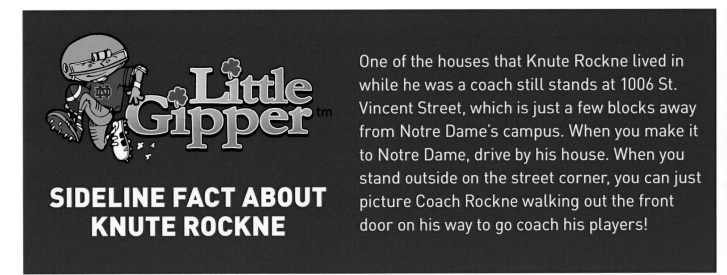

SIDELINE FACT ABOUT KNUTE ROCKNE

One of the houses that Knute Rockne lived in while he was a coach still stands at 1006 St. Vincent Street, which is just a few blocks away from Notre Dame's campus. When you make it to Notre Dame, drive by his house. When you stand outside on the street corner, you can just picture Coach Rockne walking out the front door on his way to go coach his players!

Coach Rockne
with his players

"Rock" throws a block!

Knute Rockne as a player

Knute Rockne Coaching Stats

wins—105

losses—12

ties—5

Knute Rockne & QB Gus Dorais when they were students at Notre Dame.

Gus Dorais

EXTRA TOLEDO BLADE EXTRA

Only Evening Newspaper in Toledo Receiving Associated Press News

TWO CENTS

Vol. 82—No. 77   THIRTY PAGES   TOLEDO, OHIO, TUESDAY, MARCH 31, 1931

KNUTE ROCKNE KILLED AS AIR LINER CRASHES

FRANK LEAHY
1941–1943 // 1946–1953

Frank Leahy is another coaching legend of the University of Notre Dame. He was the head coach from 1941 to 1943 and then again from 1946 to 1953. Coach Leahy was a former player on Knute Rockne's 1929 national championship team. It was reported that when Coach Leahy returned to coach Notre Dame some referred to him as "the next Knute Rockne." Coach Leahy objected, claiming "there will never be another Knute Rockne."

Well, Coach Leahy sure came close! During Coach Leahy's career at Notre Dame, he had a record of 87 wins and only 11 losses. His winning percentage of 88.7% is just short of Knute Rockne's record.

His teams won four national championships, and he coached four Heisman Trophy winners (Angelo Bertelli, Johnny Lujack, Leon Hart, and Johnny Lattner).

Although Coach Leahy was a very demanding coach, his players had lots of respect for him. After his death in 1973, several of his former players (called "Leahy's Lads") started a scholarship fund to help students that wanted to attend Notre Dame that couldn't afford it. The scholarship fund still exists today.

Coach Leahy's son and grandson would go on to play football for the Irish too!

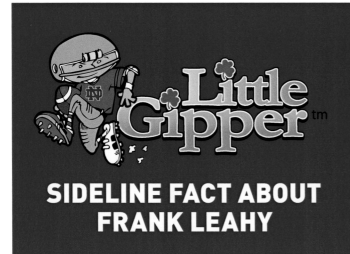

SIDELINE FACT ABOUT FRANK LEAHY

When Coach Leahy was a line coach at Fordham University, he coached a young player by the name of Vince Lombardi. Vince Lombardi would someday go on to become the great head coach of the Green Bay Packers. Notre Dame football star Paul Hornung would play for Lombardi after graduating from Notre Dame. The "Vince Lombardi Trophy"—named after Coach Lombardi—is given to the winner of the Super Bowl each year.

Coach Frank "The Master" Leahy entered the College Football Hall of Fame in 1970.

The Irish won 30-3!

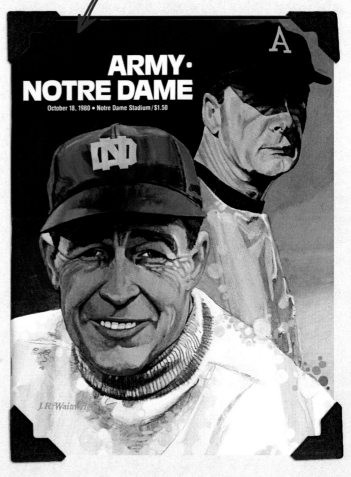

ARMY·
NOTRE DAME

October 18, 1980 • Notre Dame Stadium / $1.50

J.R.Wainwright

LUJACK and LEAHY
NOTRE DAME

Coach Leahy with Quarterback

Johnny Lujack in 1947.

Frank Leahy featured on the cover of

the Game Day Program between the

Irish and Army in 1980.

ARA PARSEGHIAN
1964–1974

Coach Parseghian talking with Quarterback Joe Theismann on the sidelines during the 1969 game between the Irish and Navy.

Notre Dame's football program struggled after Coach Leahy retired. Several head coaches were hired over the course of about 10 years, and none of them were as successful as Rockne or Leahy. Before coach Ara was hired, the Irish had five losing seasons in a row. But the "tough luck" of the Irish changed in 1964 when Coach Ara Parseghian was hired. He was the first head coach of Notre Dame that wasn't a former player on the Notre Dame football team!

Almost immediately after he became head coach, Coach Ara turned things around. The Irish won their first nine games and were ranked No. 1 heading into the final game of the season against longtime rival University of Southern California. Sadly, the Irish lost in the last two minutes of the game. During Coach Ara's 11 seasons as head coach he built a record of 95 wins, 17 losses, and 4 ties for a .836 winning percentage. His teams of 1966 and 1973 won national titles. Out of Coach Ara's 11 teams, nine of them finished the season in the Top 10 Associated Press poll.

Some of the famous players that were coached by Ara Parsigian include Heisman Trophy Winner John Huarte, and Joe Theisman. Coach Parseghian was inducted into the College Football Hall of Fame in 1980.

SIDELINE FACT ABOUT ARA PARSEGHIAN

In 1994, Coach Parseghian and his family started **The Ara Parseghian Medical Research Foundation.** The reason he started the Foundation was to raise money to help fight a very rare disease called **Niemann-Pick Type C**, a disease that took the lives of three of his grandchildren. The foundation has raised over $20,000,000 to help fight this disease! To find out more about it you can visit: **http://www.Parseghian.org**.

DAN DEVINE
1975–1980

Dan Devine on the sidelines talking with his quarterback, Joe Montana.

Dan Devine picked up right where coach Parseghian left off and continued the great tradition of Notre Dame Football. He coached at Notre Dame from 1975 to 1980. In his six seasons at Notre Dame, Coach Devine compiled a 53–16–1 record. The Fighting Irish were the 1977 national champions, led by junior quarterback Joe Montana. That championship season was completed with a huge 38–10 win in the 1978 Cotton Bowl Classic over top-ranked Texas.

Dan Devine coached several players that would go on to have great careers in the National Football League, including Joe Montana who would win four Super Bowls as the quarterback for the San Francisco 49ers. Coach Devine made the College Football Hall of Fame in 1985.

In 2002, Coach Devine died at his home in Tempe, Arizona, at age 77. Former Notre Dame head coach Lou Holtz, called Devine "a true gentleman and a tribute to the college game."

"SEND A VOLLEY CHEER ON HIGH, SHAKE DOWN THE THUNDER FROM THE SKY!"

Program from 1978 Cotton Bowl

LOU HOLTZ
1986–1996

The early 1980s were a sad period for Notre Dame Football, with the Irish unable to achieve much success after Coach Devine retired. In 1986, Lou Holtz was offered the head coaching position and immediately took it.

He turned the program around and in his first season the Irish lost five games but only by a total of 14 points. In his third season as head coach, the Irish won 12 games and went on to become the 1988 national champions.

Coach Holtz placed the now famous "Play Like a Champion Today" sign at the bottom of the stairwell at the exit of the football locker room. As the team heads out to the field for each game, each player hits the sign to remind himself to play his best!

This now famous sign is at the football locker room exit.

SIDELINE FACT ABOUT LOU HOLTZ

Coach Holtz wrote a prayer called "Team Prayer." I really like it and I think you will too.

TEAM PRAYER

This is the beginning of a new day. God has given me this day to use as I will. I can waste it or use it for good. But what I do today is important because I'm exchanging a day of my life for it.

When tomorrow comes this day will be gone forever, leaving in its place that which I have traded. I want it to be gain not loss, good not evil, success not failure.

I know I shall not regret the price I have paid for it because the future is just a whole string of now's!

Coach Holtz is the only coach in the history of college football to lead six different football teams to bowl games. He was inducted into the College Football Hall of Fame in 2008. Coach Holtz is known for his famous quotes about the game of football and about the game of life. These are some of my favorites:

"Greatness starts with belief and total commitment."

"Setbacks don't define your goals, you do."

"Perfection is possible if you accept nothing less."

LITTLE GIPPER WRAP UP

CHAPTER 1

Give yourself one "Little Gipper" Point for every correct answer then see how you did on the next page. The answers are in the back of the book in Appendix A. Visit us at our website at **littlegipper.com** and let us know how many Little Gipper Points you scored!

1. Who is the only coach in college football to take six different football teams to bowl games?

2. Which Notre Dame Coach has the highest winning percentage?

3. How many Heisman Trophy Winners were coached by Frank Leahy?

4. Who coached George Gipp and "The Four Horsemen?"

5. Which coach led the Fighting Irish to a National Championship in 1977?

6. I had "Play Like A Champion Today" painted on a sign at the locker room exit. Who am I?

7. Which Notre Dame coach played for Knute Rockne?

8. Who is the founder of the University of Notre Dame?

9. How many different coaches have won national championships for the Fighting Irish?

10. Can you name all of them?
(Give yourself two Little Gipper points if you name all of them!)

POINTS

POINTS	LITTLE GIPPER SCOREBOARD
11	Wow! You just threw a touchdown pass to beat the U.S.C. Trojans!
7–10	Great job! You just kicked a field goal to take the lead over Michigan State in the 4th quarter. I hope your defense can hold!
6–9	Terrific! You just sacked the Florida State Quarterback in the End Zone for a two-point safety!
3–5	Well done! "First and Goal" for the Irish on the Michigan 3-yard line.
0–2	Hang in There! You are just about ready to score a 1st down against Navy! Maybe go back and review Chapter 1 and try the Little Gipper Wrap Up again!

  WAY TO GO!

CHAPTER TWO

The Heisman Heroes of Notre Dame

The Heisman Trophy is an award given to the most outstanding college football player in the United States. The award has been given every year since 1935 and is probably the best known award in college sports. Notre Dame is tied with Ohio State for the most Heisman Trophy winners from one university. Here are the Heisman Heroes of Notre Dame!

SIDELINE FACT

In high school Angelo Bertelli was known as the "Springfield Rifle" because he was such a great quarterback.

Bertelli seen here running the ball against Arizona in 1941.

Lujack scores against Purdue in 1947.

IRISH

#48 ANGELO BERTELLI → 1941–1943

In 1943, Angelo Bertelli was the first Notre Dame player to receive the Heisman Trophy. Bertelli played quarterback and was called "a magician" by sportswriter Grantland Rice because of Bertelli's ability to make big plays.

#32 JOHNNY LUJACK 1943, 1946–1947 ←

When Bertelli was called into service, Coach Leahy decided to have Johnny Lujack take over the Irish offense as quarterback. Filling in for Bertelli, Lujack guided the Irish in a huge victory over Army to secure a national championship in 1943.

Starting in 1944, Lujack also began serving in the military. After fighting in World War II, he ultimately came back to Notre Dame to play for the Irish for two more seasons in 1946 and 1947. Amazingly, in both seasons the Irish won two more national championships compiling a record of 17 wins, 0 losses, and only 1 tie (to Army). Lujack won the Heisman trophy in 1947. He was named to the College Football Hall of Fame in 1960.

After graduating from Notre Dame, he went on to play for the Chicago Bears. In 1949, with the incredible Lujack in the backfield, the Chicago Bears defeated their cross-town rival, the Chicago Cardinals, with Lujack setting a new NFL passing record of 468 yards and six touchdowns.

The 1943 Irish football team was packed with talent. Not only did Bertelli win the Heisman, but also two of his teammates (Creighton Miller and Jim White) finished in the top 10 Heisman Trophy voting!

The same year he won the Heisman (his senior year), he got called into the military to help fight World War II. He actually only completed six games that year due to his military service. In 1972 Angelo Bertelli joined the College Football Hall of Fame.

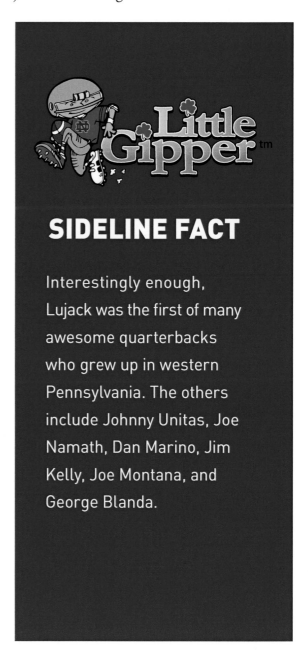

SIDELINE FACT

Interestingly enough, Lujack was the first of many awesome quarterbacks who grew up in western Pennsylvania. The others include Johnny Unitas, Joe Namath, Dan Marino, Jim Kelly, Joe Montana, and George Blanda.

#82 LEON HART
➤ 1947–1949

Leon Hart was an offensive end for the Fighting Irish (and another great player from western Pennsylvania!). He won the Heisman in 1949 and to this day is one of only two linemen to receive the trophy.

Hart had no idea what it felt like to lose in an Irish uniform. During his career Notre Dame went 36-0-2 and claimed three national championships. It must be a Hart family rule to play for the Irish because both Leon's son and grandson played for them!

After his flawless college career, Hart went on to play with the Detroit Lions for eight seasons. During that time the Lions won three NFL titles. Leon Hart was inducted into the College Football Hall of Fame in 1973.

"WHAT THOUGH THE ODDS BE GREAT OR SMALL, OLD NOTRE DAME WILL WIN OVER ALL!"

Leon Hart, 1949 Heisman Trophy Winner, posed in action inside Notre Dame Stadium.

#14 JOHNNY LATTNER

1951–1953

Johnny Lattner started his Irish career in 1951 as the halfback for Notre Dame. He won the Heisman Trophy as a senior in 1953 in the final year of Coach Leahy's time as head coach.

At the age of 78 he is still going strong! He is still dedicated to the mission of the University. For example, he is known for lending out his Heisman Trophy to raise money for various charities. As Mr. Lattner recently said, "What

better way than to use [the trophy] for charity than have it sit around my house."

After his career with Notre Dame, he went on to play for the Pittsburgh Steelers. But his time with the team was limited because he joined the U.S. Air Force after his first season. A career-ending injury to the knee made it so he could never play football again. Johnny Lattner entered the College Football Hall of Fame in 1979.

Lattner escapes a Trojan tackler in 1953.

"Superman" Lattner flying inside Notre Dame Stadium in 1952.

SIDELINE FACT

As a Senior he returned eight kickoffs for 321 yards and two touchdowns (that's an average of over 40 yards per return)!

Lattner gearing up for the game.

Leahy's Lads

JOHNNY LATTNER

LEON HART

JOHNNY LUJACK

ANGELO BERTELLI

FRANK LEAHY AND HIS FOUR
HEISMAN TROPHY WINNERS.

#5 PAUL HORNUNG

1954–1956

Paul Hornung (pronounced Horn-ing) is probably considered one of the best all-around athletes in Notre Dame History. He is the only player to ever win the Heisman trophy while playing for a losing team (the Irish had two wins and eight losses in 1956).

Originally a halfback and fullback during his first season with the Irish, he eventually became the starting quarterback for his last two seasons. Not only was Hornung a great runner, passer, and offensive threat, he also had kicking duties and was one of the most accurate kickers of his time. Hornung also played defense and led his team in pass break-ups and finished second in tackles and interceptions his senior season. No wonder his nickname was "Golden Boy!"

Hornung was the No. 1 draft pick for the Green Bay Packers and went on to have a great career under Coach Vince Lombardi. He would go on to win four league championships with the Packers, including the first ever Super Bowl in January 1967 against the Kansas City Chiefs. Paul was inducted into the College Football Hall of Fame in 1985.

> "WHILE HER LOYAL SONS ARE MARCHING ONWARD TO VICTORY!"
>
> —THE NOTRE DAME VICTORY MARCH

SIDELINE FACT

Hornung is still a huge supporter of the University of Notre Dame and its football program. In 2000, he sold his Heisman Trophy for $250,000 to fund scholarships at Notre Dame!

Hornung hands off the ball against Miami in 1955.

Paul Hornung runs with the ball.

#7 JOHN HUARTE
→ 1962–1964

John Huarte was Notre Dame's sixth Heisman Trophy winner and played quarterback at Notre Dame when Ara Parseghian was head coach. His senior year the Irish finished 9–1 (only losing to USC) and were declared national champions in several polls. John set 12 Irish records his senior year!

After his football days at Notre Dame, he went on to play professionally for several teams including the Jets and the Patriots. He is now a successful businessman in California. John Huarte joined the College Football Hall of Fame in 2005.

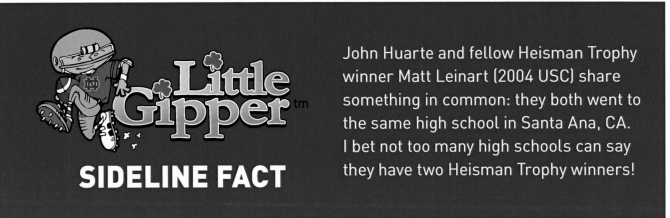

Little Gipper™

SIDELINE FACT

John Huarte and fellow Heisman Trophy winner Matt Leinart (2004 USC) share something in common: they both went to the same high school in Santa Ana, CA. I bet not too many high schools can say they have two Heisman Trophy winners!

#81
TIM BROWN
→ 1984-1987

Tim Brown won the Heisman Trophy in 1987 and is the most recent winner from Notre Dame. He was the first wide receiver to win the Heisman and did so by a large amount (611 points!). Not only was he a fantastic athlete, he was also a very intelligent player. In fact, Coach Holtz said that Tim Brown was "[t]he most intelligent player I've ever been around."

During his senior year at Notre Dame, Tim Brown averaged almost 22 yards each catch! He was also a huge threat as a kickoff and punt returner. In an early game in his senior season at Notre Dame Stadium, Tim had an amazing game against Michigan State when he returned back-to-back punt returns for touchdowns (66 yards and 71 yards).

Tim was drafted by the Oakland Raiders as their number one pick in the 1988 NFL Draft. He played for the Oakland Raiders for fifteen years, before retiring in 2004 from the Tampa Bay Buccaneers. He was selected to play in multiple Pro Bowls. "Touchdown Timmy" made the College Football Hall of Fame in 2009.

Today, Tim is involved in many charitable causes. For example, he is the National Chairman of "911 For Kids", an organization that teaches kids about how to be prepared to deal with emergency situations. You can learn more about this great organization and Tim's work by visiting **http://www.911forkids.com**.

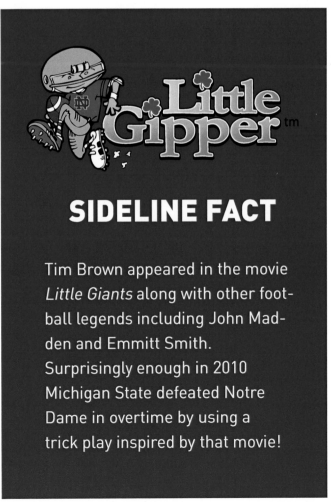

SIDELINE FACT

Tim Brown appeared in the movie *Little Giants* along with other football legends including John Madden and Emmitt Smith. Surprisingly enough in 2010 Michigan State defeated Notre Dame in overtime by using a trick play inspired by that movie!

LITTLE GIPPER WRAP UP

CHAPTER 2

You know what to do! Good luck!

1. How many Heisman Trophy winners are from Notre Dame?

2. Ok, can you name all of them? (give yourself three Little Gipper points if you can name all of them)

3. I was called a "magician" by sportswriter Grantland Rice. Who am I?

4. I sold my Heisman trophy to raise money for Notre Dame scholarships. What is my name?

5. Who is the most recent player from Notre Dame to win the Heisman Trophy?

6. I am one of only two linemen to have ever won the Heisman Trophy. What's my name?

7. I was a quarterback, played for Coach Parseghian, and won the Heisman Trophy. Do you remember my name?

8. I was the first player from Notre Dame to win the Heisman Trophy. Who am I?

9. I lend my Heisman Trophy to raise money for charities. What is my name?

10. Which Heisman Trophy winner led the Irish to a huge victory over Army in 1943?

POINTS

	LITTLE GIPPER SCOREBOARD
12	A flawless performance! You just completed 12 out of 12 passes and scored a touchdown to secure a last minute victory over Army!
9–11	Very impressive! You ran for a two-point conversion to give the Irish the lead over Texas with only two minutes to go!
6–8	Great job! You tackled the running back from Ohio State for a loss!
3–5	Nice! You just completed a 7-yard pass on first down!
0–2	I know you are trying hard! I'm sure you will get that first down on your next try.

 WAY TO GO!

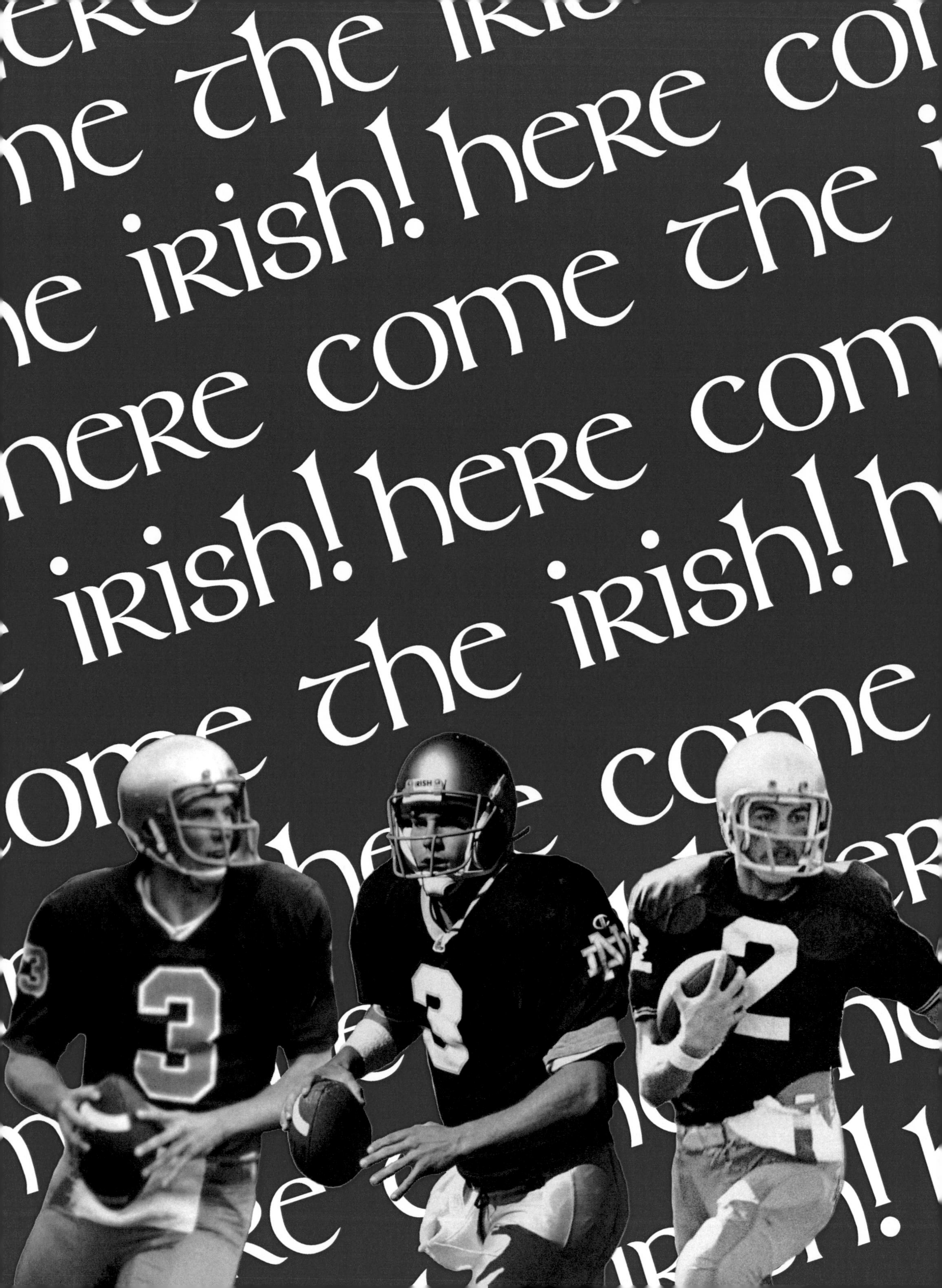
here come the irish!

CHAPTER THREE

All-Americans, Hall of Famers & Record Setters

Notre Dame has produced more All-Americans than any other football program. Also, there are more players and coaches from Notre Dame in the College Football Hall of Fame than from any other school. Please refer to the Appendix for more information!

In the rest of this chapter I've included additional information about just some of these All-Americans, Hall of Famers, and others that hold records for the Irish.

GEORGE GIPP
1917–1920

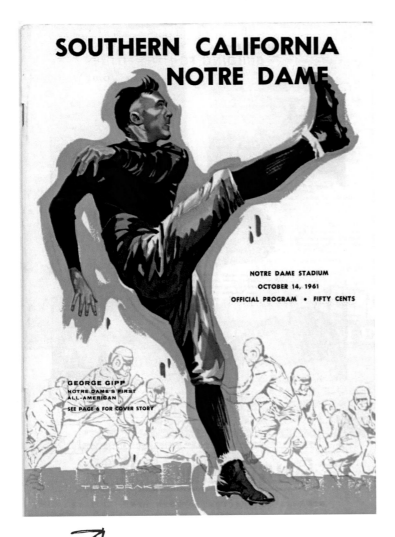

SOUTHERN CALIFORNIA
NOTRE DAME

NOTRE DAME STADIUM
OCTOBER 14, 1961
OFFICIAL PROGRAM • FIFTY CENTS

GEORGE GIPP
NOTRE DAME'S FIRST
ALL-AMERICAN
SEE PAGE 6 FOR COVER STORY

TED DRAKE

George "The Gipper" Gipp is probably the most well-known player in the history of Notre Dame Football. He was an outstanding athlete and football player. He could run, pass, punt, and play defense. He led the Irish in rushing and passing in three seasons (1918, 1919 and 1920). Gipp was also a fantastic defensive player and apparently never allowed a pass completion in his territory.

Tragically, Gipp was hospitalized with strep throat a few days after the Notre Dame vs. Northwestern game on November 20, 1920. He never recovered and died a few weeks later on December 14, 1920.

Irish legend has it that on his deathbed he spoke his last words to Coach Rockne. Gipp's last words became the basis for Coach Rockne's "Win One for The Gipper" motivational speech to his team in 1928 when the Irish defeated their arch rival Army 12–6 in an historic game played at the Polo Grounds in New York. "The Gipper" was inducted into the College Football Hall of Fame in 1951.

1961 Program for the USC v. Notre Dame game featuring ND's first All-American, George Gipp. The Gipper would have been proud of the Irish that day as they shut out the Trojans, 30–0.

"WIN ONE FOR THE GIPPER!"

Gipp punts the ball against arch-rival Army in 1917.

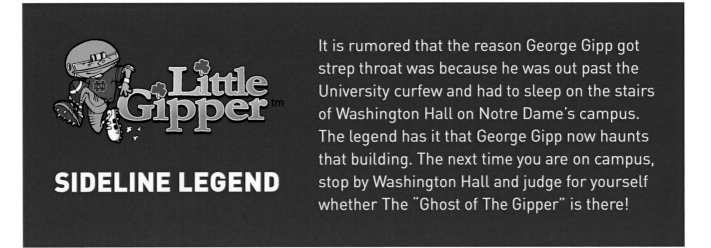

Little Gipper™

SIDELINE LEGEND

It is rumored that the reason George Gipp got strep throat was because he was out past the University curfew and had to sleep on the stairs of Washington Hall on Notre Dame's campus. The legend has it that George Gipp now haunts that building. The next time you are on campus, stop by Washington Hall and judge for yourself whether The "Ghost of The Gipper" is there!

THE FOUR HORSEMEN
1924

Miller, Layden, Crowley, and Stuhldreher pictured on their horses!

The Four Horsemen are probably the most well-known backfield in the history of college football. It all began when Coach Rockne placed Harry Stuhldreher at quarterback, Jim Crowley at left halfback, Don Miller at right halfback, and Elmer Layden at fullback.

After Notre Dame's 13-7 victory over Army on October 18, 1924, sportswriter Grantland Rice for the *New York Herald-Tribune* wrote this creative description for the dominant Notre Dame backfield:

"Outlined against a blue, gray October sky the Four Horsemen rode again. In dramatic lore they are known as famine, pestilence, destruction, and death. These are only aliases. Their real names are Stuhldreher, Miller, Crowley, and Layden."

After that story ran, the players were photographed seated on horseback, wearing their uniforms and holding footballs. That photograph was published across the country and guaranteed the long-lasting fame of the group.

The Four Horsemen might be the greatest backfield ever to have played in college. They played 30 games together as a backfield unit and only lost to one team, Nebraska, twice. All four players eventually were elected to the College Football Hall of Fame—Layden in 1951, Stuhldreher in 1958, Crowley in 1966, and Miller in 1970.

The Four Horsemen are a huge part of Irish football history. Here they appear on the game day ticket against USC in 1999.

JOE MONTANA
1975–1979

Joe Montana earned the nickname "The Comeback Kid" and "Cool Joe" because of all of the come-from-behind victories he led the Irish to during his career. He led the Irish to become national champions in 1977. In his final year and last game ever for Notre Dame, Montana rallied the Irish past Houston in the Cotton Bowl for a stunning 35–34 victory.

"Cool Joe" went on to have an incredible career with the San Francisco 49ers, winning four Super Bowls and being named the Most Valuable Player in two of them.

SIDELINE FACT

The Comeback Kid picked up with the 49ers right where he left off with the Irish. In the 1982 NFC Championship game at Candlestick Park in San Francisco, Montana led the trailing 49ers on a 90-yard drive at the end of the 4th quarter to beat the Dallas Cowboys, 28-21, on their way to win Super Bowl XVI. A four-year-old Tom Brady was in the stands that day. Tom Brady himself would become a legendary quarterback, winning three Super Bowls with the New England Patriots as of 2012.

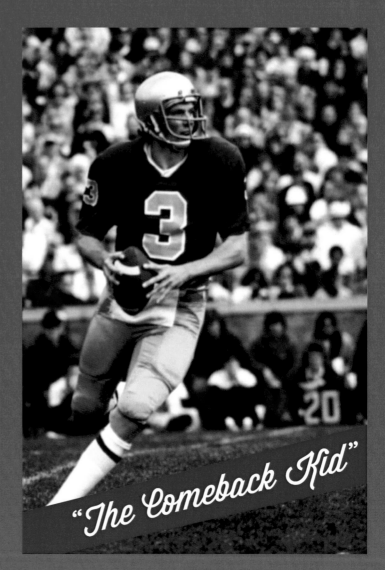

"The Comeback Kid"

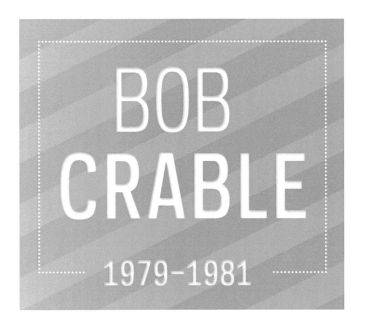

One of the most feared linebackers in Irish history. He had 521 career tackles and was a two time All-American. He holds the record for the most tackles in a game with 26 vs. Clemson in 1979. Crable also holds the record for the most tackles in a season (187 in 1979).

QB Ralph Guglielmi was a unanimous All-American in 1954. He also made the College Football Hall of Fame in 2001. He completed 208 career passes for 3,073 yards and 18 touchdowns. He is pictured here in a 1953 game against North Carolina.

RICK MIRER

1989–1992

Rick Mirer was a great quarterback and leader of the Irish. He finished his career at Notre Dame 1st in career touchdowns and 2nd all time for total offense, completions, and passing yards. In his final game at Notre Dame Stadium he was brilliant in leading the Irish to a come-from-behind victory against Penn State.

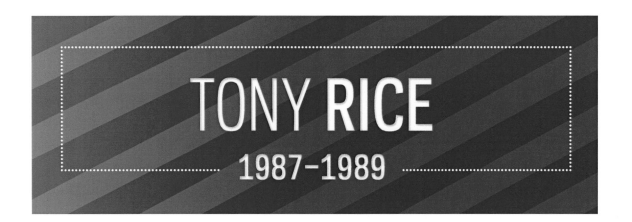

TONY RICE
1987–1989

Tony Rice is the only quarterback to lead the Irish to a perfect season of 12 wins. That year (1988), the Irish were named national champions. Tony was an outstanding runner and ran coach Holtz's offense to perfection. I had the opportunity to meet Mr. Rice at the USC v. Notre Dame football game in October 2011. He was very kind and encouraging. When I told him I was a quarterback of my football team he gave me a "high 5" and said, "Well, Jake, us quarterbacks have to stick together!" I'll never forget that.

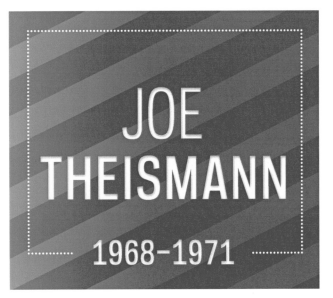

JOE THEISMANN
1968-1971

In 1969, as a junior, Joe Theismann led the Irish to a No. 5 ranking and their first bowl appearance in 45 years. The next year Theismann and the Irish ended the season with a 10–1 record, a No. 2 ranking and a victory over Texas in the Cotton Bowl. To this day, he still holds the record for most passing yards in a game (526 vs. USC in 1970). Joe went on to have a very successful pro career and led the Washington Redskins to victory in Super Bowl XVII in 1983. Also, in 1982 Joe was named the NFL's "Man of the Year" for his dedication to the health and welfare of children. Joe Theismann was inducted into the College Football Hall of Fame in 2003.

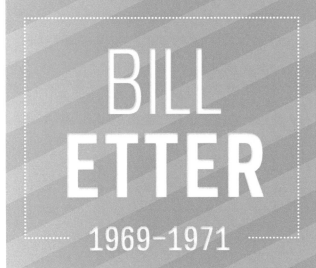

BILL ETTER
1969-1971

Bill Etter is from my hometown of Spokane, WA. Bill was a quarterback for the Irish. He still holds the record for the most rushing yards by a Notre Dame quarterback in a single game (146 yards vs. Navy in 1969). Bill also was the first Notre Dame Player to receive the ABC-TV "Player of the Game" Award.

JEROME BETTIS

1991–1993

"The Bus"

Nicknamed "The Bus" (which was given to him by the Notre Dame student newspaper), he had an incredible college and pro career. At Notre Dame, Bettis finished his career with 1,912 rushing yards (5.7 yards per carry), and caught 32 passes for 429 yards (13.4 yards per reception). He was the MVP of the 1992 Sugar Bowl when he rushed for 150 yards and three touchdowns to lead the Irish to a 39–28 upset of #3 Florida. He went on to have a great pro career for the Los Angeles Rams and the Pittsburgh Steelers.

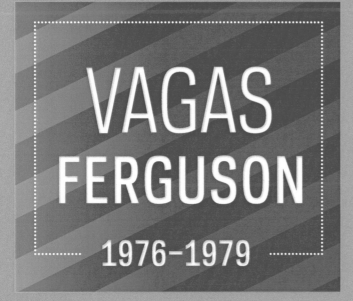

VAGAS FERGUSON

1976–1979

When Vagas Ferguson finished his Irish career, he was the all-time leading ground gainer with with 3,472 rushing yards and 32 touchdowns. He received offensive MVP honors in the 1978 Cotton Bowl with 100 yards rushing and three touchdowns in a 38–10 win over the Texas Longhorns.

MICHAEL FLOYD

2009-2012

Michael Floyd was an amazing wide receiver. He is the Notre Dame career record holder for receptions (271), receiving yards (2,686), receiving touchdowns (37), average yards receiving per game (85.7) and games with at least 100 receiving yards (17). In 2012, he was drafted in the first round of the NFL Draft by the Arizona Cardinals. He is the first Notre Dame wide receiver to be drafted in the first round of the NFL Draft since Tim Brown.

KEN MACAFEE

1974-1977

Known as a "bruising" tight end because of his strength and size. He was a huge target for Joe Montana and helped lead the Irish to their 10th National title in 1978! Ken caught 128 career passes for 1,759 yards and 15 TDs.

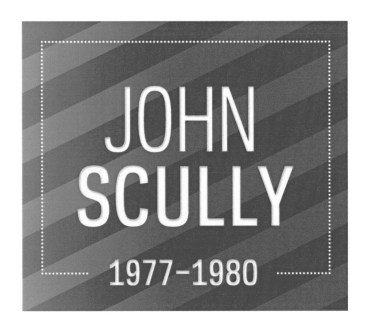

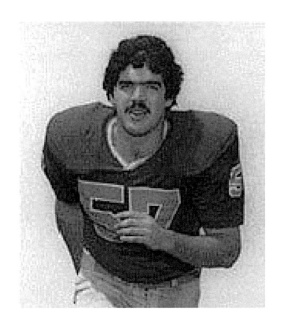

A great lineman for the Irish and then the Atlanta Falcons. One very interesting fact about John is that he is a creative musician, writing two very well known songs about Notre Dame. The first is "Here Come the Irish" and the second is "Our Lady of The Lake." You can purchase "Here Come the Irish" from www.ndcatalog.com. I always like to listen to "Here Come the Irish" before Notre Dame football games.

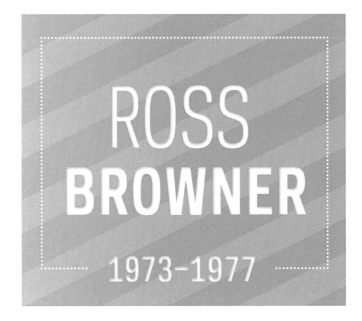

Ross Browner was certainly one of the best defensive players of all time for the Irish. He made 340 career tackles, broke up ten passes, recovered eight fumbles, blocked two kicks, scored two safeties, and even scored a touchdown! He was a consensus All-American in 1976 and 1977 and was also the UPI and AP "Lineman of the Year" in those same years. He was inducted into the College Football Hall of Fame in 1999.

BOB GOLIC
1975–1978

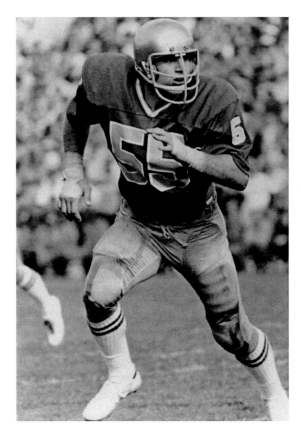

Bob Golic was a punishing linebacker for the Irish and a member of the 1977 national championship team. He was a unanimous All-American pick as the senior captain for the Irish in 1978.

MICHAEL ORIARD
1968–1970

Michael Oriard is the only "walk on" player (meaning he was not offered a scholarship) in school history to become a starter, team captain, and second-team All-American. He played center, snapping the ball to both Terry Hanratty and Joe Theismann. After he graduated from Notre Dame he wrote many books, including *The End of Autumn*, which tells the story of his life at Notre Dame. My dad and I read that book together and I highly recommend it. Dr. Oriard (he is a professor at Oregon State University) grew up in my hometown of Spokane and attended my (future) high school, Gonzaga Prep!

ALAN PAGE

1964–1966

Alan Page (#81) was a fearsome defensive end who had 63 tackles in 1966 to help lead the Irish to a national championship. He piled up 134 career tackles, recovered four fumbles, broke up two passes, and scored one touchdown during his career with the Irish. Interestingly, he is now a judge on the Minnesota Supreme Court! Alan Page entered the College Football Hall of Fame in 1993.

CHRIS ZORICH
1988-1990

Chris Zorich was a fantastic nose guard for the Irish. He was a starting player on Coach Holtz's 1988 championship team. His hard work earned him All-American status in 1989 and 1990. He went on to play seven seasons in the NFL before returning to Notre Dame to obtain his law degree.

"Notre Dame, our Mother, Tender, strong & true, Proudly in the heavens, Gleams thy gold & blue...

RON POWLUS
1994-1997

Ron Powlus was a two-time captain who set 20 school records as the Notre Dame starting quarterback. He started all 44 regular-season games (plus two bowl games) in which he played and completed 558 of 969 passes for 7,602 yards and 52 TDs.

...Glory's mantle cloaks thee, Golden is thy fame, & our hearts forever, Praise thee, Notre Dame."

BOB WILLIAMS

ALLEN PINKETT

Bob Williams quarterbacked the Irish to a national championship on Coach Leahy's 1949 national championship team. He played for the Irish from 1948 to 1951.

Allen Pinkett was a great running back and played from 1982 to 1985. He left Notre Dame as the all time leading rusher with 4,131 yards. He was the first player in Notre Dame history to rush for 1,000 or more yards in three consecutive seasons.

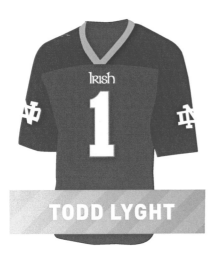

TODD LYGHT

JUSTIN TUCK

BRADY QUINN

Todd Lyght was a defensive cornerback on Coach Holtz's 1988 national championship team and played for the Irish from 1987 to 1990. He was a two-time All-American selection and made 11 career interceptions, one of which was returned for a touchdown.

Justin Tuck was a fantastic defensive end for the Irish from 2001 to 2004. His nickname was "The Freak" because he was so powerful and fierce. He compiled 43 tackles for losses and 13.5 sacks while at Notre Dame. Both of those are school records.

Brady Quinn was a quarterback for the Irish from 2003 to 2006. He holds the most records of any Notre Dame quarterback, including for the most completions in a career (929), most passing yards in a season (3,919), and most career touchdown passes (95), to name just a few.

MICHAEL STONEBREAKER

RAGHIB ISMAIL

Michael Stonebreaker was a key defensive player on Coach Holtz's 1988 championship team. Is there a better last name for a linebacker than "Stonebreaker?" Ouch! He led the Irish in tackles in 1990 with 95. He was a two time consensus All-American and a unanimous first team selection in 1990.

"The Rocket" was an explosive kickoff and punt returner. He was a two-time All-American for the Irish and finished second in the race for the Heisman Trophy behind BYU's Ty Detmer in 1990. In the next chapter, you will read about how "The Rocket" returned two kickoff returns for touchdowns to help the Irish beat Michigan!

JEFF SAMARDZIJA

JIMMY CLAUSEN

GOLDEN TATE

Jeff Samardzija (also known as "The Shark") was a great wide receiver for the Irish from 2003 to 2006. But his true passion was in baseball and he is now a pitcher for the Chicago Cubs.

Jimmy Clausen was also a great quarterback and he played from 2007 to 2009. He finished his career as a "top 10" quarterback in many record categories. He holds the record for the most completions in a game (37 vs. Navy in 2009), the most completions per game in a career (19.5), and the highest completion percentage in a season (67.4%).

Golden Tate played wide receiver for Notre Dame from 2007 to 2009. He won the 2009 Biletnikoff Award as the top wide receiver in college football after breaking Jeff Samardzija's records for career receptions and receiving yards.

LITTLE GIPPER WRAP UP

CHAPTER 3

You are a pro on what to do at this point. Get out there and score some for the Little Gipper! OK, it's time for another series of questions. Keep track of your score! Good luck!!

1. I led Notre Dame in both rushing and passing in 1918, 1919, and 1920. Who am I?

2. As a backfield we played 30 games together and only lost to one team. Who are we?

3. They call me the "Comeback Kid." Who am I?

4. I am the only quarterback to lead the Irish to a perfect 12–0 season. Who am I?

5. My nickname is for a vehicle that gets launched into outer space. Who am I?

6. I still hold the record for the most rushing yards in a single game by a Notre Dame quarterback. What is my name?

7. I wrote two songs about Notre Dame. What is my name and what are the names of the songs? (Give yourself three points if you get all of them!)

8. My nickname is for something that you might ride to school everyday. What's my name?

9. I threw for 526 yards against USC in 1970. Who am I?

10. I was drafted in the first round of the NFL draft in 2012. What's my name?

POINTS

12
9–11
6–8
3–5
0–2

LITTLE GIPPER SCOREBOARD

Wow! You just completed a 50-yard "Hail Mary" pass to beat Michigan in overtime.

Terrific! You just returned an interception for a touchdown in the 1st quarter against Boston College.

Bravo! You just completed a 15-yard pass to give the Irish a 1st down and goal to go on Purdue's 5 yard line!

You just found out that you are going to be starting quarterback against the Pittsburgh Panthers next Saturday!

Keep trying hard! You will definitely improve if you keep with it.

WAY TO GO!

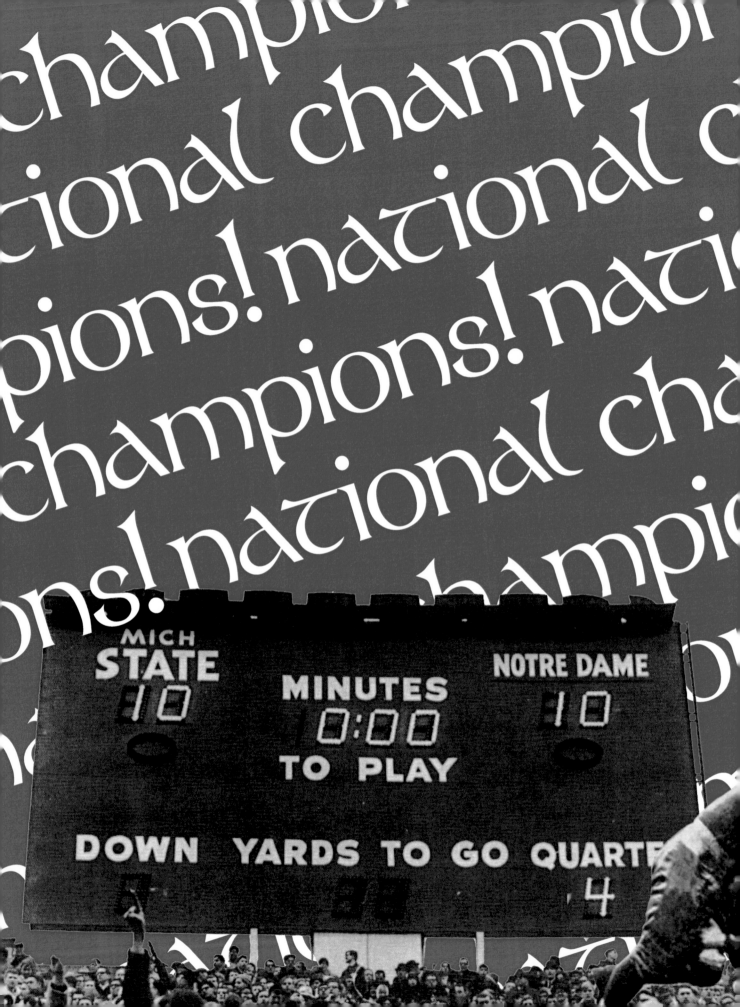

CHAPTER FOUR

Magical Seasons and Miracle Moments

THE EXIT FROM THE NOTRE DAME LOCKER ROOM BACK THEN...

Notre Dame has had many magical seasons since it fielded its first football team in 1887. Perhaps the most magical seasons are the 11 years they have won the national title!

Here are posters and other items celebrating some of those championship seasons!

1924

1929

NOTRE DAME

Notre Dame 14	
Indiana 0	
	Notre Dame 26
	Georgia Tech. 6
Notre Dame 14	
Navy 7	Notre Dame 19
	Drake 7
Notre Dame 19	
Wisconsin 0	Notre Dame 26
	Northwestern 6
Notre Dame 7	Notre Dame 13
Carnegie Tech. 0	Southern California 12
	Notre Dame 7
	Army 0

ND
1929

NATIONAL CHAMPIONS

1943

1947

PLAY LIKE
A CHAMPION
TODAY!

1949

1966 Notre Dame

Larry Conjar

Fighting Irish

Bob Bleier

Nick Eddy

Offense

Ara Parseghian

Terry Hanratty   Coley O'Brien

Gmitter   Bob Kuechenberg   Dick Swatland   George Goeddeke   Tom Regner   Paul Seiler   Jim Seymour

Defense

Rhoads   Pete Duranko   Mike McGill   John Pergine   Jim Lynch   John Horney   Kevin Hardy   Dave Martin   Alan Page

Tom O'Leary   NATIONAL   Tom Schoen   CHAMPIONS   Jim Smithberger

IRISH

1966

NOTRE DAME   FIGHTIN' IRISH
NATIONAL CHAMPIONS
1973

1973

1988

There are so many great and historic moments in Notre Dame Football history that it is challenging to pick the most memorable. Luckily, back in 1999 Notre Dame Fans were given an opportunity to vote on what they thought were the best moments in Notre Dame history over the last century. Here they are!

#20 NOTRE DAME vs. FLORIDA *1992 Sugar Bowl*

The #18 Irish were trailing #3 Florida by five in the final 11 minutes of the game. In a 4th quarter shootout, Jerome "The Bus" Bettis scores three rushing touchdowns to send Notre Dame back to South Bend as Sugar Bowl Champions. Notre Dame 39, Florida 28.

The Bus

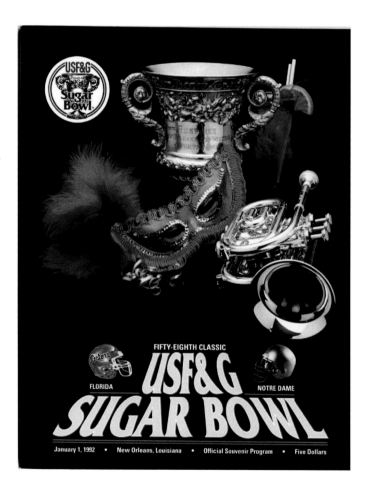

1992 Sugar Bowl Game Day Program. The Irish beat the Gators behind the solid offense of Jerome Bettis.

MICHIGAN SEPT. 20, 1980

Sec. Box Row Seat

EAST SIDE BOX SEAT $14.00

1980 Notre Dame Tri-Captains,

47 57 27

Bob Crable, John Scully, Tom Gibbons

$14.00

GATE

Sec. Box Row Seat

MICHIGAN vs. NOTRE DAME

SAT., SEPT. 20 · 1:30 P.M. EST
NOTRE DAME STADIUM
NON REFUNDABLE

EAST SIDE BOX SEAT

Notre Dame was facing its long-time rival Michigan in a regular season game in Notre Dame stadium. In the final 41 seconds the Irish were losing 26–27 and had 80 yards to go for a touchdown. Freshman quarterback Blair Kiel led the Irish down the field into Michigan territory. For the final play of the game Harry Oliver kicked a 51-yard field goal to lead the Irish to a victory, 29–27.

Oliver boots the Irish to victory!

#18   NOTRE DAME vs. ALABAMA *1975 Orange Bowl*

The Alabama Crimson Tide were undefeated heading into the Orange Bowl on New Year's Day. In what would turn out to be a defensive game, Notre Dame stopped Alabama late in the 4th quarter with an interception by Reggie Barnett. Coach Parseghian was carried off the field in honor of his great career and final game as the Irish head coach. Notre Dame won 13–11.

#17   NOTRE DAME vs. W. VIRGINIA *1989 Fiesta Bowl*

Ticket to Fiesta Bowl Game

Heading into this game, both teams were untied and undefeated. While many thought that West Virginia would win, Notre Dame made it not even close. Tony Rice and his offense along with solid help from the likes of Chris Zorich and Michael Stonebreaker on defense helped bring home the national title to the Irish for the first time in 11 seasons. The Irish won 34–21.

Coach Ara during his last season as head coach.

Coach Holtz on the sidelines during the West Virginia game.

Coach Holtz and Tony Rice together on the sidelines

#16 NOTRE DAME VS. TEXAS *1978 Cotton Bowl*

The #1 ranked Texas Longhorns were thought to be unstoppable. Texas was led by the Heisman Trophy winning running back, Earl Campbell. The Associated Press favored the Longhorns and said the game would be "a one sided mismatch." The Associated Press turned out to be only partially correct. The game was a one sided mismatch, but it was Notre Dame who came out on top. With Joe Montana and Vagas Ferguson leading the offense, and Ross Browner and Bob Golic leading the defense, the Irish took home their 10th National championship winning the contest 38–10.

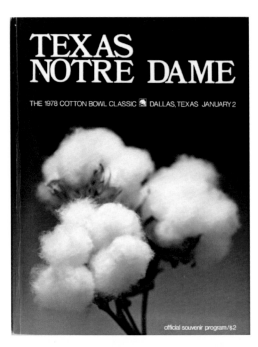

#15 NOTRE DAME VS. ARMY *Nov. 1946*

In 1946, the Army Cadets were the two-time defending national champions. In the 1944 and 1945 seasons, the Irish were crushed by Army by a combined score of 107–0! In 1946, Army had two Heisman Trophy winners on their team, Doc Blanchard and Glenn Davis. But the Irish had future Heisman Trophy winner Johnny Lujack. Lujack was amazing. He ran, passed, punted, recovered fumbles, and played solid defense. In fact, he made a game saving tackle on Doc Blanchard. The game ended in a 0–0 tie. At the end of the season, the Irish were crowned national champions.

ARMY ★ NOTRE DAME ★ 1946

Football Program for the Cadets vs. the Irish historic battle. This cover features an Army Cadet in uniform.

Lujack makes game-saving tackle for the Irish

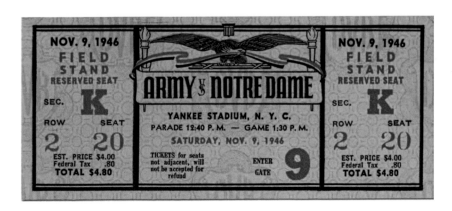

The completion of one of the startling "Dorais to Rockne" passes which beat the Army in 1913 and modified the entire game of football. Here's Knute making a touchdown.

Rockne running for a touchdown against Army in 1913.

More than perhaps any other game, this one put Notre Dame on the football map. Their fearless coach, Jesse Harper signed up for his team to travel to New York to play mighty Army for the first time in history. And what a magical game it was! Quarterback Gus Dorais and a young tight end by the name of Knute Rockne displayed what the "forward pass" could do. The Army Cadets were helpless to defend against this new way of moving the ball. All of Notre Dame's five touchdowns that day came from pass plays. One of the game referees that day said that he always thought it was possible to play the game that way, but "had never seen the forward pass developed to such a state of perfection." Notre Dame won the game easily, 35–13. Thanks to Gus and Knute for all that they did that day.

"Snow Bowl"

#13 NOTRE DAME vs. PENN ST. *Nov. 1992*

It was a cold and snowy day in South Bend. And the Irish were finding themselves in quite a hole at the very end of the 4th quarter. The Nittany Lions of Penn State were ahead 16–9 with only two minutes to play. Rick Mirer, Jerome Bettis, and Reggie Brooks teamed up to drive the Irish down to a 4th down and goal on the Penn State four yard line with 25 seconds left in the game. Bettis caught a touchdown pass on the next play to pull the Irish within one point. The Irish decided to go for the two-point conversion—and the win. Rick Mirer dropped back, scrambled, and found Reggie Brooks in the corner of the end zone to pull out the 17–16 win. The Irish prevailed in what was called "The Snow Bowl."

Reggie Brooks battles the snow and the Penn State Nittany Lions. Brooks' two-point conversion would win the game for Irish.

Michigan State had just come off of a big win over the USC Trojans and headed to South Bend to take on the Irish and Tim Brown. Things started off badly for the Spartans when the Irish scored a safety on the opening kickoff, but that did not even compare to what would soon happen. Tim Brown would go on to return two punt returns for touchdowns as the Irish rolled over the Spartans, 31–8.

RESERVED SEAT

27 41 5
Sec. Row Seat

GATE **MICHIGAN STATE** vs.
14 **NOTRE DAME**
Sat., Sept. 19, 1987
Kick-off time to be announced
Notre Dame Stadium
$20.00 Non Refundable

100th ANNIVERSARY
NOTRE DAME
The Spirit of Legends
F·O·O·T·B·A·L·L
1887 1987

Game Day ticket

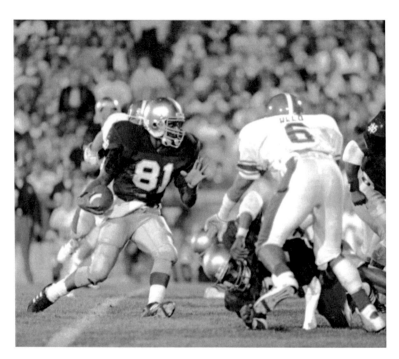

Tim Brown scored more points all by himself than the entire Michigan State team that day.

"And our hearts forever, love thee Notre Dame."

Mishawaka News

The South Bend Tribune.

CLASSIFIED ADS

SECTION THREE   SOUTH BEND, INDIANA, SUNDAY MORNING, NOVEMBER 17, 1957.   39   SECTION THREE

IRISH DEFENSE SHATTERS SOONER STREAK

Going into this game the Sooners had won 47 straight games, including a 40–0 win over the Irish the year before at Notre Dame Stadium. The Sooners' last loss happened on September 26, 1953 to none other than Notre Dame! Many people believed the highly-favored Sooners were obviously going to win this 1957 match-up, which was a home game for Oklahoma. In fact, in the most recent edition of Sports Illustrated published before the game, the Sooners were featured on the cover with the magazine stating "Why Oklahoma Is Unbeatable."

The Irish defense played outstandingly and held the Sooners to 145 yards total offense. Notre Dame's running back Dick Lynch scored the game's only touchdown to break the longest winning streak in college football history! The Irish won 7–0.

Dick Lynch scores to snap Sooners' 47 game winning streak!

1957 Football Program for the Irish vs. Sooners match-up.

#10 NOTRE DAME vs. ALABAMA *1973 Sugar Bowl*

Going into this game, coach Paul "Bear" Bryant's Alabama team was ranked No. 1 in the AP poll, and had an undefeated season. While Alabama was ranked No. 1, Notre Dame was in the top five. The game was a classic battle. With a narrow lead of one point, the Irish took possession of the ball on their 1-yard line with only minutes left. On 3rd down, if the Irish did not convert, they would have been forced to punt. But, Tom Clements completed a 35 yard pass that gave Notre Dame the chance to run out the clock. The Irish won 24–23.

#9 NOTRE DAME vs. MICHIGAN ST. *Nov. 1966*

The Fighting Irish were ranked No.1 and the Spartans were ranked No. 2. Interestingly enough, this game was the first time ever since the AP poll was created that No. 1 met No. 2 in a football game. Going into that game Notre Dame had the highest average score per game with 36.2. But, Michigan State had a great defense led by Bubba Smith. It was a grueling and grinding game that ended up in a 10–10 tie. Notre Dame would move on to defeat USC 51–0 the next week. The Irish were named national champions that year!

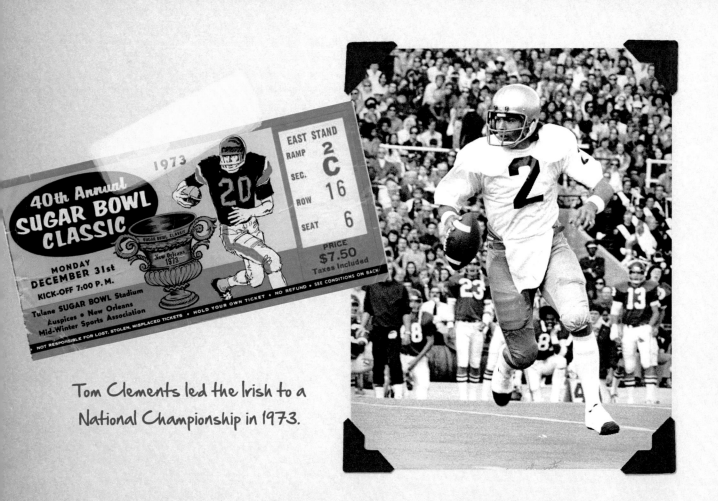

Tom Clements led the Irish to a National Championship in 1973.

Scoreboard at the end of the MSU game.

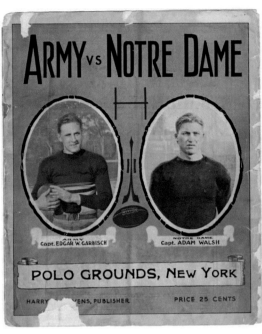

This game is significant in Notre Dame history not just because the Irish beat Army, but for what happened after the game. Heading into this contest, Notre Dame had won 47 out of its last 51 games and Army had only lost two games in the last two seasons. The game was played in New York at the Polo Grounds, which is where the New York Giants baseball team played. It was a hard-fought victory for the Irish, whose backfield performed magically. After Notre Dame's 13–7 victory, a sportswriter by the name of Grantland Rice was so amazed by the Irish backfield that he named them "The Four Horseman" in an article the day after the game. The Irish went on to win the National Championship that year.

NOTRE DAME vs. MICHIGAN *Sept. 1989*

The No. 1 ranked Irish and the No. 2 ranked Wolverines met at Michigan Stadium on this cold and rainy fall day. The Irish were just coming off of a 12–0, national championship season. The Wolverines were Big 10 and Rose Bowl Champions the year before. The Notre Dame defense led by Chris Zorich held Michigan scoreless until the second half. But the Irish were led to victory by the lightning fast Raghib "Rocket" Ismail who returned two kickoffs for touchdowns in the 2nd half. Notre Dame won 24–19.

"The Game of the Century"
NOTRE DAME vs. OHIO ST. *Nov. 1935*

#6

This was the first time these two teams would meet, and it would be a terrific game. Over 81,000 fans watched the game at Ohio Stadium and another eight million listened on their radios. The Irish were 5–0 and coached by Elmer Layden, one of the famed "Four Horsemen." The Buckeyes were 4–0 and averaged 50 points per game! The sports editor for the Columbus Evening Dispatch predicted that the Irish would fall to the Buckeyes 36–0. He turned out to be incredibly wrong. The Irish were down 13–0 in the fourth quarter but rallied to pull within one point, 13–12. The Irish had the ball on the Ohio State 49 yard line with only one minute remaining. Quarterback Bill Shakespeare hit tight end Wayne Miller for the game winning score with just seconds to go. Notre Dame won, 18–13. In 1969, this contest was named the "Game of the Century" by a panel of Associated Press voters.

A scene from the "Game of the Century" in 1935

The "Green Jersey" Game
NOTRE DAME vs. USC Oct. 1977

This football game was named the "Green Jersey" game because it was the first time since 1963 when Notre Dame had worn green jerseys. Coach Dan Devine wanted to inspire the Irish so he secretly placed the green jerseys in their lockers before the game.

Notre Dame just dominated the USC Trojans! Quarterback Joe Montana threw two touchdown passes and threw for 167 yards. The Irish won 49–19. That year the Irish would go on to win the national championship game beating Texas in the Cotton Bowl.

SOUTHERN CAL • NOTRE DAME
October 22, 1977 • Notre Dame Stadium • $2.00

The cover to the Game Day Program for the "Green Jersey" game featured Knute Rockne, Frank Leahy, Ara Parseghian, and Dan Devine.

Students gather around the "Trojan Horse" that was rolled out at Notre Dame Stadium. Since 1926, the Irish and the Trojans have met on the football field every year, except for three years during World War II. It is one of the best-known rivalries in all of college football.

Cool Joe

"Win One for the Gipper"

NOTRE DAME vs. ARMY *Nov. 1928*

#4

This is the game against Army where Coach Rockne delivered his famous "Win One for the Gipper" speech to inspire his players to win the game in honor of Notre Dame great, George Gipp. Army was heavily favored to beat the Fighting Irish in Yankee Stadium that day. There were more than 78,000 people on hand to watch the contest. Coach Rockne's speech really worked and Notre Dame won 12–6.

Johnny O'Brien catches the ball and scores the game-winning touchdown for Notre Dame.

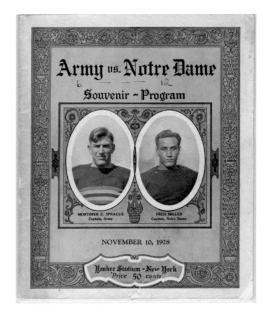

#3 NOTRE DAME vs. FLORIDA ST. *Nov. 1993*

This game featured another historic matchup between the No. 1 and No. 2 ranked teams in the country. The Seminoles traveled to South Bend with a 16-game winning streak, a victory over cross-state rival Miami, and a No. 1 ranking. The Irish came into the game 9–0 and also hunting for the national championship. Coach Holtz knew he had his hands full with the 'Noles. They averaged 44.3 points per game, and were led by future Heisman Trophy winning quarterback, Charlie Ward. It was a back and forth battle with both teams trading touchdowns, one after the other. For the first time in 23 games Florida State found themselves losing at halftime. With the score 31–24 with 51 seconds remaining in the game, QB Charlie Ward drove his team to the Irish 14 yard line with ten seconds left to play. Thanks to defensive end Shawn Wooden, who knocked down the ball, Notre Dame was victorious.

Game Day Ticket to the match-up against FSU. Edward "Moose" Krause is pictured on the ticket. He was a longtime athletic director and coach at Notre Dame.

Fans storm the field at Notre Dame Stadium as the Irish beat Florida State 31-24.

"Chicken Soup Game"
NOTRE DAME vs. HOUSTON *1979 Cotton Bowl*

Joe Montana was literally "Joe Cool" that day. The icy cold weather in Dallas sent Montana to the locker room at halftime with hypothermia and the Irish trailing 20–12. With only 7:37 left in the game Houston had a commanding lead of 34–12 and all seemed hopeless for the Irish.

But that didn't stop Montana. He ran for one touchdown, threw for one, and threw for a couple of two-point conversions as the Irish came back to win 35–34 on the final play of the game. As former Notre Dame football star Paul Hornung said at the end of the television broadcast, "Montana has done it again!"

Ticket to what would later be called the "Chicken Soup" game. Joe Montana warmed up at half time with chicken soup.

Joe Montana saves the day as he leads the Irish to one last come-from-behind victory. Montana was known as "The Comeback Kid" because of his ability to lead his team to several victories after trailing in the 4th quarter.

The Hurricanes came into this game unstoppable. They had won 36 straight games. They had also embarrassed the Irish recently beating them 58–7 and 24–0. No school had a better record over the previous five seasons then Miami's 56–9 record. The Irish took a quick 14–0 lead, but the 'Canes recovered and the score was tied at halftime 21–21. The Irish got the better of Miami in the 2nd half, and led 31–24. But the 'Canes recovered a Tony Rice fumble on the Irish 14 yard line with 2:10 remaining. On 4th down and seven yards to go, Miami QB Steve Walsh threw a touchdown pass to a diving Miami receiver. The score was 31–30. The Hurricanes who, "always play to win," according to their head coach Jimmy Johnson, went for the two-point conversion. But Miami came up short when Notre Dame's Pat Terrell broke up Walsh's pass. The Irish celebrated their 31–30 victory like never before. Tony Rice appeared on the cover of Sports Illustrated the following week with the headline, "NOTRE DAME IS BACK." The magazine was certainly right as Notre Dame finished the season with a perfect 12–0 record and won the national championship.

OCTOBER 15, 1988

NOTRE DAME · MIAMI

JOHN LATTNER
1953 – HEISMAN TROPHY WINNER

Game Day Program for the ND vs. Miami game featuring Heisman Trophy Winner Johnny Lattner.

Pat Terrell saved the day for the Irish when he broke up the two-point conversion pass in the end zone to seal the victory against Miami.

LITTLE GIPPER WRAP UP

CHAPTER 4

Little Gipper Points await you! Go for it!

1. I batted down a pass on a two-point conversion play to help the Irish beat the Miami Hurricanes. Who am I?

2. I "booted" the Irish to victory over the Michigan Wolverines in 1980. Who am I?

3. I made a game-saving tackle against Army in 1946. What's my name?

4. I was carried off the field after the Irish won the 1975 Orange Bowl. Who am I?

5. I caught many passes from my quarterback, Gus Dorais, to help Notre Dame beat Army in 1913. Who am I?

6. I scored a touchdown to help the Irish break the longest winning streak in college football history. Who am I and what team did the Irish beat? (Give yourself two points if you get both answers correct).

7. Who scored the winning two-point conversion for the Irish in the "Snow Bowl?"

8. I returned two punts to help the Irish beat Michigan State in 1987. Who am I?

9. The Irish beat which team in which bowl to end the season a perfect 12 wins and 0 losses?

10. What was the last year the Irish won a national championship?

POINTS

11
7–10
3–6
0–2

LITTLE GIPPER SCOREBOARD

Huge congratulations! You just scored a touchdown on a 99-yard kick-off return to beat Alabama! The Irish are headed to a BCS bowl game!

Super job! You just recovered a fumble in the end zone to give the Irish a three-point lead over Stanford. Two minutes left in the game so hold strong against the Cardinal!

Well done! You just kicked a 45-yard field goal to take the lead over Nebraska in the 2nd Quarter!

That's OK! Maybe try reviewing this chapter again!

   WAY TO GO!

CHAPTER FIVE

The Notre Dame Experience

Notre Dame Football is about more than just the coaches, players, and the games. It is also about the traditions and stories of this great college and its campus. Here are some of my favorite things about Notre Dame.

The GOLDEN DOME

THE NOTRE DAME EXPERIENCE

The most recognizable and famous landmark on campus is the Main Building, topped with the Golden Dome and a giant 19- foot statute of Mary, the mother of Jesus, watching over her University. The dome is actually painted with real gold!

SIDELINE FACT

One legend I heard is that if you want to attend the University of Notre Dame, you should never walk up the front steps of the Main Building or you won't get accepted to attend! So, make sure that if you visit the Main Building you go inside through the doors that are found beneath the main steps. Better to be safe than sorry!

NOTRE DAME STADIUM

Aerial view of Notre Dame Stadium before the historic Notre Dame vs. Miami match-up in 1988.

Notre Dame Stadium is probably the most famous college football field in the country. It is nicknamed "The House That Rockne Built" because Knute Rockne was responsible for leading the effort to build a stadium that could fit more and more Irish fans.

Work started on the Stadium in April 1930 and it opened four months later for the first game of what would tragically be Knute Rockne's last season with the Irish.

Since the 1966 season every Irish home game has been a sellout, with the exception of a Thanksgiving Day matchup with Air Force in 1973.

In the 1990s, a massive renovation of the Stadium took place, adding 20,000 new seats, a new press box, new scoreboards, and lots of other items. Amazingly, The House That Rockne Built is still carefully preserved inside the new stadium, which can hold 80,795 fans.

SIDELINE SUGGESTION

When you go to a game at Notre Dame Stadium, get there early (at least an hour) so you can experience all of the pre-game activities. One fun thing you might try is climbing to the very top row and walking all the way around the perimeter of the stadium to experience great views of the campus (and all of the tailgaters below!)

Also, make sure to check and see if you can get a tour on the Friday before the game. When you walk down the tunnel toward the field, you can just picture the roar of Irish fans watching Paul Hornung, Johnny Lattner, Joe Montana, and many other Notre Dame greats battling on the turf!

A ticket to the 1997 game "rededicating" Notre Dame Stadium after it was expanded. The Irish beat the Yellow Jackets of Georgia Tech 17–10.

THE FIGHTING IRISH
and
THE LEPRECHAUN

THE NOTRE DAME EXPERIENCE

The exact history of Notre Dame's "Fighting Irish" nickname may never be known. It became a popular name for the Irish football team in the 1920s. Originally, it was meant as an insult to the many young Irish Catholics that played for Notre Dame. What started out as an insulting term became a source of pride for the Irish football squad. The Fighting Irish nickname was made official in 1927 by Notre Dame president Father Matthew Walsh.

Beginning in about 1930, Irish terrier dogs served as mascots for Notre Dame (that's why you see some of the early coaches and players pictured with terriers). In 1965, the Leprechaun became the official mascot and has been ever since.

"The Bus" celebrates with The Leprechaun on the sidelines.

The Notre Dame
MARCHING BAND

THE NOTRE DAME EXPERIENCE

The Irish Guard as pictured on the ticket to the 1973 game between the Irish and the Trojans. The members of the Irish Guard act as the protectors of the marching band.

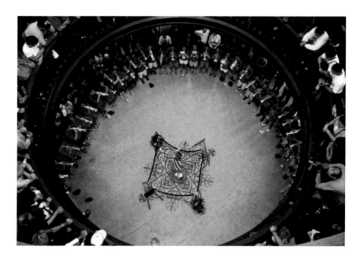

"Trumpets under the Dome" on Friday night before the Pittsburgh vs. Notre Dame in 2002.

Notre Dame has the oldest marching band in the country. Watching the marching band play both before and during a home game is a great experience and incredibly inspirational. When you attend a home game, make sure you go to "Trumpets under the Dome", which is where the trumpet players gather underneath the Golden Dome of the Main Building to play the Notre Dame Victory March and Notre Dame, Our Mother. Try getting inside the building about 30–45 minutes before the performance so you can find a good location on the second floor just above the trumpeters. I guarantee you won't be disappointed! (But remember, don't walk up the outside main staircase—use the inside one!)

Marching Band playing at the Tennessee vs. Notre Dame in 2001.

HESBURGH LIBRARY

Named in honor of long-time president of the University, Rev. Theodore Hesburgh, C.S.C., the Hesburgh Library's mural of Jesus (officially named "The Word of Life") is often referred to as "Touchdown Jesus" by fans. With arms raised, it looks like Jesus is signaling another touchdown for the Irish! When the Hesburgh Library was opened in 1963, it was the largest college library in the world.

Father "FAIR CATCH" CORBY

Rev. William Corby, C.S.C. was one of the early presidents of the University. Fr. Corby was present during the infamous Battle of Gettysburg during the American Civil War and blessed the Irish Brigade before they went into battle. The statue of him blessing the troops is found on that battlefield in Pennsylvania and a replica was placed on the Notre Dame campus in 1911.

The statue is referred to as "Fair Catch Corby" because with his one arm raised he looks like he is signaling for a "fair catch."

As you can tell, Notre Dame Fans see football signs in all kinds of places!

HERE COME THE IRISH!

THE BASILICA
of the
SACRED HEART

No trip to Notre Dame would be complete without visiting the Basilica. It is the tallest structure on campus and is an amazing church, both inside and out. On Saturday home football games, the players attend mass at the Basilica and then walk down to the Stadium to the cheers of Notre Dame Fans!

THE GROTTO

The Grotto is right next to the Basilica, and it is a quiet place where you can go light a candle and pray. Every night I stayed on the campus at the Morris Inn when I was there for football camp, we walked up to the Grotto for some quiet time. We were very thankful we had an opportunity to be at this historic place.

Nighttime at the Grotto.

HELMET PAINTING

I think this was definitely one of the coolest traditions in college sports, the painting of the University of Notre Dame football helmets. Before 2011, every Monday night (it used to be on Friday nights) during the football season, a group of students painted the game day helmets inside Notre Dame Stadium. What's amazing is that the gold for the helmets actually came from the Golden Dome. During the "regilding" process, gold was actually removed from the Golden Dome. That gold was then mixed with additional gold paint and used on the helmets. I bet those Irish helmets were the most expensive in college football! In 2011, the new gold helmets are no longer painted.

"RUDY" THE MOVIE

THE NOTRE DAME EXPERIENCE

Chances are, you have already seen this great movie. It is based on the life story of Rudy Ruettiger, who wanted to go to Notre Dame and play football since he was a young boy. But everybody told him he was too small, or too slow, or not smart enough to go to Notre Dame. Rudy proved them all wrong. With incredible hard work Rudy got into Notre Dame, made the football team as a walk on, and ultimately ended up on the field for the last game of the 1975 season against Georgia Tech...and helped sack the quarterback! It's a great story filmed right on the campus of Notre Dame.

Rudy is now a motivational speaker and author. He always reminds people that you can accomplish anything you set your mind to!

Ticket to the 1993 world premiere of the movie *Rudy* at the Morris Civic Auditorium in South Bend.

Rudy (#45) being carried off the field by his teammates after the Irish beat Georgia Tech.

KNUTE ROCKNE, ALL AMERICAN

THE NOTRE DAME EXPERIENCE

Speaking of movies filmed on campus, you should definitely get a copy of this movie. It tells the story about Knute Rockne's life and the part of George Gipp is played by a young actor named Ronald Regan, the future President of the United States. I find it really interesting that President Reagan's nickname for the rest of his life was "The Gipper."

1988 postage stamp featuring Coach Knute Rockne. He worked for the postal service before he was a student at Notre Dame.

In 1988, Coach Knute Rockne was honored with his image being placed on a postage stamp. President Ronald Reagan, pictured above, celebrated the event at the University.

YOUTH FOOTBALL CAMP

THE NOTRE DAME EXPERIENCE

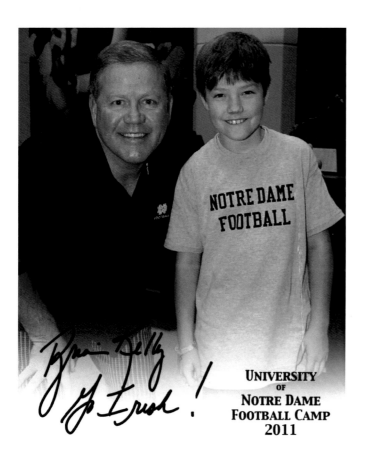

Another great tradition about Notre Dame is its football summer camps run by the coaches and by several of the players. If you have a chance to attend one, you should definitely go. These camps teach you about how to play the game, but they also emphasize how important it is to work hard, get good grades, and to be a good person. I can't wait until the next time I can go!

At every youth football camp, the campers form the "ND" logo at the Knute Rockne entrance to Notre Dame Stadium.

Coach Brian Kelly and me at the ND Summer Camp, 2011.

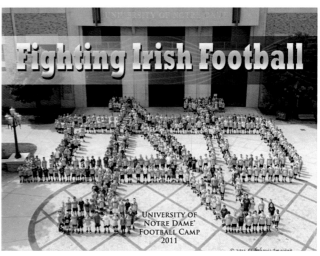

Photos courtesy Lighthouse Imaging

THE SHIRT PROJECT

This is another great Notre Dame tradition. The Shirt Project began when a Notre Dame student decided to make a t-shirt that students could wear to show their "unity" at a home football game against Michigan in 1990. Over 9,000 t-shirts were sold for that game. The idea caught on and now it is an annual tradition! Money raised from all the sales of "the shirt" goes to great causes like helping Notre Dame students who have lots of medical bills and to other students that may not be able to afford such things as textbooks.

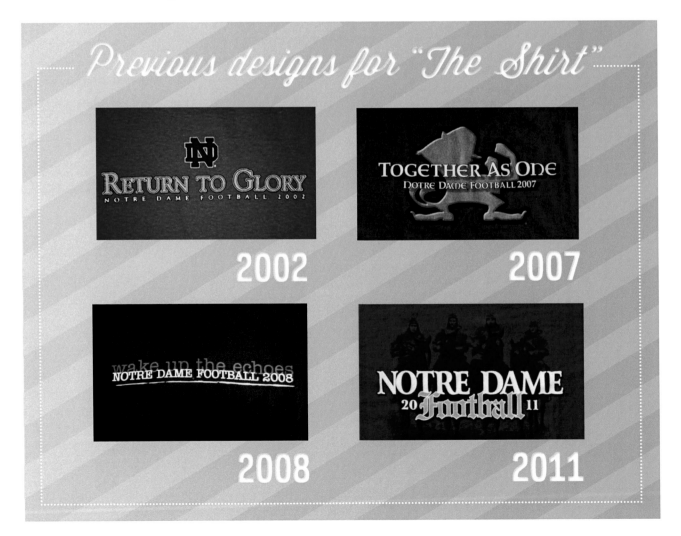

Previous designs for "The Shirt"

RETURN TO GLORY
NOTRE DAME FOOTBALL 2002
2002

TOGETHER AS ONE
NOTRE DAME FOOTBALL 2007
2007

wake up the echoes
NOTRE DAME FOOTBALL 2008
2008

NOTRE DAME
20 Football 11
2011

DEBARTOLO PERFORMING ARTS CENTER

Another one of the great buildings on Notre Dame's campus is the DeBartolo Performing Arts Center. It was opened in 2004 and has five different concert halls where all sorts of musical and theater performances take place. I highly recommend you take a tour of this amazing building if you can. Ask to see the hall where the big pipe organ is located. When you go back stage you will see they have a "Play Like A Champion Today" sign to inspire the musical performers!

HAMMES BOOKSTORE

THE NOTRE DAME EXPERIENCE

Not far from the DeBartolo Performing Arts Center you will find the Hammes Bookstore. It was built in 1998 and is an incredible building filled with books, apparel, jewelry and all sorts of other Notre Dame merchandise. It even has a great café. During football weekends the Hammes Bookstore is always filled with many students, fans, and visitors. When you make your way to the University, make sure to stop by! If by some chance you cannot make it there in person, check it out online at http://www.ndcatalog.com.

"There's a magic in the sound of their name. Here come the Irish of Notre Dame."

LITTLE GIPPER WRAP UP

CHAPTER 5

Now, let's see how many "LG" Points you can score!

1. What year was Notre Dame Stadium built?

2. Can you name two films that were actually filmed on Notre Dame's campus?

3. What future U.S. President played the part of George Gipp in the film *Knute Rockne, All-American*?

4. What's the tallest structure on campus?

5. The football helmets are painted with gold that comes from where?

6. What happened to Notre Dame Stadium in 1997?

7. Who is shown on the front of the Hesburgh Library?

8. A statue of who is on top of the Golden Dome?

9. How many different halls are in the DeBartolo Performing Arts Center?

10. What is the name of the prayerful cave-like place next to the Basilica?

POINTS LITTLE GIPPER SCOREBOARD

POINTS	
10	Most excellent! You just won the Orange Bowl against Florida!
6–9	Terrific! You just ran for a touchdown against Oklahoma!
3–5	Very good! You made a tackle to keep Illinois from making a first down!
0–2	I am proud of your efforts! Don't ever give up!

 WAY TO GO!

LITTLE GIPPER FINAL WRAP UP

I really hope you have enjoyed this book about Notre Dame Football. Now, add up all of your Little Gipper Points from Chapters 1-5 and see how you did!

50-56 POINTS—An outstanding performance! You just helped the Irish win their next national championship! And, it was against USC! You will have a great career after you graduate from UND!

40-49 POINTS—Fantastic work! You just led the Irish to a victory in the Cotton Bowl over Oklahoma State! You finished the season 10-1. A national championship may be close at hand...

30-39 POINTS—An admirable performance! The Irish had a very good season with 8 wins and 5 losses, including a bowl victory thanks to all of your efforts!

20-29 POINTS—You had a winning season. I bet you will get selected for a bowl appearance!

10-19 POINTS—Things are looking up for you! Next year you will no doubt improve! Good luck and keep with it!

0-9 POINTS—It was a rebuilding year for you! Hang in there and keep doing what Coach Rockne would do: Don't give up and keep trying your hardest! I'm proud of your efforts.

ANSWERS TO LITTLE GIPPER WRAP UP QUESTIONS

Chapter 1

1. Lou Holtz

2. Knute Rockne

3. Four (Bertelli, Lujack, Hart, Lattner)

4. Knute Rockne

5. Dan Devine

6. Lou Holtz

7. Frank Leahy

8. Fr. Edward Sorin

9. Five

10. Knute Rockne, Frank Leahy, Ara Parseghian, Dan Devine, Lou Holtz

Chapter 2

1. Seven

2. Bertelli, Lujack, Hart, Lattner, Hornung, Huarte, Brown

3. Angelo Bertelli

4. Paul Hornung

5. Tim Brown

6. Leon Hart

7. John Huarte

8. Angelo Bertelli

9. Johnny Lattner

10. Johnny Lujack

Chapter 3

1. George Gipp

2. The Four Horsemen

3. Joe Montana

4. Tony Rice

5. Raghib "The Rocket" Ismail

6. Bill Etter

7. John Scully. The songs are "Here Come The Irish" and "Our Lady of The Lake."

8. Jerome "The Bus" Bettis

9. Joe Theismann

10. Michael Floyd

Chapter 4

1. Pat Terrell

2. Harry Oliver

3. Johnny Lujack

4. Coach Ara Parseghian

5. Knute Rockne

6. Dick Lynch. University of Oklahoma

7. Reggie Brooks

8. Tim Brown

9. West Virginia in the 1989 Fiesta Bowl

10. 1988

Chapter 5

1. 1930

2. *Knute Rockne, All American* and *Rudy*

3. Ronald Reagan

4. The Basilica of The Sacred Heart

5. The Golden Dome

6. It was significantly updated and expanded to hold many more football fans.

7. "Touchdown Jesus"

8. Mary, the mother of Jesus

9. There are five different performance venues.

10. The Grotto

ACKNOWLEDGEMENTS

During the process of writing this book, many people helped me in so many ways. I am very thankful for everything these people have done for me. I want to say a huge "Little Gipper" thank you to all of them! This book would not have been possible without all of these great people:

• Sue Shidler and the staff of the Hammes Bookstore;

• Ellen Eide for her amazing talent on the graphic design of this book. Ellen graduated from Notre Dame in the Spring of 2012;

• Michael Low and his team in the University Licensing Department (for letting me use the University logos in this book);

• Elizabeth Hogan in the University Archives for all of her hard work in gathering the photos;

• Professor Emeritus Jim Langford (now President of Corby Press) for his advice throughout this project; and

• Wendy Harmon and her team at the Collegiate Licensing Company.

I also want to thank all of the people who allowed me to use their pictures (or pictures of their family members) or other items in this book:

Tom Clements

Chris Zorich

Joe Theismann

Paul Hornung

Johnny Lujack

Jerome Bettis

Johnny Lattner

Justice Alan Page

Patrick Terrell

Ken MacAffee

Ralph Guglielmi

Vagas Ferguson

Ara Parseghian
(and his assistant Peg Romano)

Dan Devine Jr.

Don Padgett

John Scully

Rudy Ruettiger
(and his assistant Carol Cummings)

Michael Floyd

Lou Holtz

Ross Browner

Tony Rice

Karen and Bob Golic

Ron Powlus

John Oliver

Lisa and Bob Crable

Tim Brown
(and his assistant Elise Kim)

Bill Etter

The family of Gus Dorais

Ryan Leahy

John Huarte

Michael Bertelli

The family of Knute Rockne

Brian Kelly

The family of Leon Hart

The family of George Gipp

The families of "The Four Horsemen"
(Miller, Layden, Crowley & Stuhldreher)

Joe Montana

Rick Mirer

Dr. Michael Oriard

Reggie Brooks

The family of Dick Lynch

Lighthouse Imaging

The Notre Dame Shirt Committee

I want to thank all of my teachers who continue to influence my life in so many ways: my Montessori school teachers Lael Sheahan, Mike McConkey and Joan McLean; Mrs. Lisa Bennett from Cataldo Catholic School; my piano teacher Mrs. Barbara Miller who has instructed me since I was five years old; and Mr. Pat Herbers, my chess coach. I want to thank my basketball coach, Nicole Duvernay. Finally, I want to thank my football coaches who are teaching me about this great game of football: Coach Tom McKeirnan, Tim Mitrovich, Mark Russell, Scott Scelfo, and Rob Burnett.

APPENDIX: NOTRE DAME PLAYERS AND COACHES IN THE COLLEGE FOOTBALL HALL OF FAME

NAME	SCHOOL	POSITION	YEARS	INDUCTED
Hunk Anderson	Notre Dame	Guard	1918–1921	1974
Angelo "Springfield Rifle" Bertelli	Notre Dame	Quarterback	1941–1943	1972
Tim Brown	Notre Dame	Wide Receiver	1984–1987	2009
Ross Browner	Notre Dame	Defensive End	1973, 1975–1977	1999
Jack Cannon	Notre Dame	Guard	1927–1929	1965
Frank Carideo	Notre Dame	Quarterback	1928–1930	1954
George Connor	Holy Cross, Notre Dame	Tackle	1942–1943, 1946–1947	1963
Jim "Sleepy Jim" Crowley	Notre Dame	Halfback	1922–1924	1966
Zygmont "Ziggy" Czarobski	Notre Dame	Tackle	1942–1943, 1946–1947	1977
Dan Devine	Arizona State, Missouri, Notre Dame	Coach	1955–1980	1985
Bob "Grandpappy" Dove	Notre Dame	End	1940–1942	2000
Ray "Iron Eich" Eichenlaub	Notre Dame	Fullback	1911–1914	1972
Bill "Moose" Fischer	Notre Dame	Tackle/Guard	1945–1948	1983
George "The Gipper" Gipp	Notre Dame	Halfback	1917–1920	1951
Jerry "Boomer" Groom	Notre Dame	Center	1948–1950	1994
Ralph "Goog" Guglielmi	Notre Dame	Quarterback	1951–1954	2001
Jesse Harper	Notre Dame, Alma, Wabash	Coach	1906–1917	1971
Leon Hart	Notre Dame	End	1946–1949	1973
Frank "Nordy" Hoffmann	Notre Dame	Guard	1930–1931	1978
Lou Holtz	William & Mary, North Carolina State, Arkansas, Minnesota, Notre Dame, South Carolina	Coach	1969–2004	2008
Paul "The Golden Boy" Hornung	Notre Dame	Quarterback	1954–1956	1985
John Huarte	Notre Dame	Quarterback	1962–1964	2005
Johnny Lattner	Notre Dame	Halfback	1951–1953	1979
Elmer "The Thin Man" Layden	Notre Dame	Fullback	1922–1924	1951
Frank "The Master" Leahy	Boston College, Notre Dame	Coach	1939–1953	1970
Johnny Lujack	Notre Dame	Quarterback	1943, 1946–1947	1960
Jim Lynch	Notre Dame	Linebacker	1964–1966	1992
Ken MacAfee	Notre Dame	Tight End	1974–1977	1997
Jim "Jungle Jim" Martin	Notre Dame	End/Tackle	1946–1949	1995
Bert Metzger	Notre Dame	Guard	1928–1930	1982
Creighton Miller	Notre Dame	Halfback	1941–1943	1976
Don Miller	Notre Dame	Halfback	1922–1924	1970
Edgar "Rip" Miller	Notre Dame	Tackle	1922–1924	1966
Fred Miller	Notre Dame	Tackle	1926–1928	1985
Wayne "Double L" Millner	Notre Dame	End	1933–1935	1990
Alan Page	Notre Dame	Defensive End	1964–1966	1993
Ara Parseghian	Miami (OH), Northwestern, Notre Dame	Coach	1951–1974	1980
Knute "Rock" Rockne	Notre Dame	Coach	1918–1930	1951
Louis "Red" Salmon	Notre Dame	Fullback	1900–1903	1971
Marchy Schwartz	Notre Dame	Halfback	1929–1931	1974
William Shakespeare	Notre Dame	Halfback	1933–1935	1983
Red "Six-Yard" Sitko	Notre Dame	Halfback/Fullback	1946–1949	1984
John "Clipper" Smith	Notre Dame	Guard	1925–1927	1975
Harry "Stuly" Stuhldreher	Notre Dame	Quarterback	1922–1924	1958
Joe Theismann	Notre Dame	Quarterback	1968–1970	2003
Adam "Ad" Walsh	Notre Dame	Center	1922–1924	1968
Bob "Bobby" Williams	Notre Dame	Quarterback	1948–1950	1988
Tommy Yarr	Notre Dame	Center	1929–1931	1987
Chris "Zorro" Zorich	Notre Dame	Defensive Tackle	1987–1990	2007

BIBLIOGRAPHY

Books

Heisler, John. *100 Things Notre Dame Fans Should Know & Do Before They Die*. Chicago, Illinois: Triumph Books, 2009.

Holtz, Lou. *Wins. Losses, and Lessons*. New York, New York: HarperCollins, 2006.

Oriard, Michael. *The End of Autumn*. Garden City, New York: Doubleday, 1982.

Vonada, Damaine. *Notre Dame The Official Campus Guide*. Notre Dame, Indiana: University of Notre Dame Press, 1998.

Walters, John. *Notre Dame Golden Moments 20 Memorable Events That Shaped Notre Dame Football*. Nashville, Tennessee: Rutledge Hill Press, 2004.

Wolfe, Rich. *For Notre Dame Fans Only The New Saturday Bible*. United States: Lone Wolfe Press.

Websites

Killoren, Connor. "Notre Dame Football: The 50 Best Players in Fighting Irish History." October 13, 2011 <http://bleacherreport.com/articles/890170-notre-dame-football-the-50-best-players-in-school-history>

http://www.collegefootball.org

http://www.und.com

http://www.heisman.com

http://www.bleacherreport.com